THE POWER OF DAD WORKBOOK

The Influence Of Today's Fathers And The Destiny Of Their Children

BRIAN PRUITT

Copyright © 2008 by Brian Pruitt

The Power Of Dad Workbook
The Influence Of Today's Fathers And The Destiny Of Their Children
by Brian Pruitt

Printed in the United States of America

ISBN 978-1-60477-745-1

All rights reserved solely by the author. The author guarantees all contents are original and do not infringe upon the legal rights of any other person or work. No part of this book may be reproduced in any form without the permission of the author. The views expressed in this book are not necessarily those of the publisher.

Unless otherwise indicated, Bible quotations are taken from The Holy Bible, New International Version. NIV, Copyright © 1973, 1978, 1984 by International Bible Society. Used by permission of Zondervan Publishing House, and the Scripture Quotations noted The Message, Copyright © 1993, 1994, 1995, 1996, 2000, 2001, 2002. Used by permission of NavPress Publishing Group, and Verses marked KJV are taken from The King James Version of the Bible.

www.xulonpress.com

Table Of Contents

CHAPTER 1 9
What Is The Power Of Dad

CHAPTER 2 17
Powerful Roots

CHAPTER 3 23
Powerful Memories, Mirrors & Mentors

CHAPTER 4 31
The Power of Being Absent
- Who's Your Daddy?

CHAPTER 5 35
The Power of Being There
- Identity

CHAPTER 6 41
The Power of Communication and Apologies

CHAPTER 7 47
Kryptonite and Superman

CHAPTER 8 51
The Power of the Prodigal

CHAPTER 9 ....**55**
The Power of Love

CHAPTER 10 ....**61**
The Fight of Your Life

CHAPTER 11 ....**65**
Following & Fighting

ABOUT THE AUTHOR **69**

**BRIAN PRUITT MOTIVATIONAL PRODUCT
PROMOTINAL PAGE** **71**

**BRIAN PRUITT MOTIVATIONAL CONTACT
INFORMATION PAGE** **73**

This Workbook works best when used with The Power of Dad Book Written By: Brian Pruitt

How to use and get the most out of this workbook:
Read a chapter in The Power of Dad Book, then answer the questions and do the exercises in the same chapter in The Power Dad Workbook.

CHAPTER ONE

What Is The Power Of Dad

Webster's definition of the word father is pretty simple:
Father: The male parent, an ancestor, our fathers before us, an originator. Ultimately our personal definition of the word father will determine how we father our children. So let me ask you, how do you define the word Father?

Describe the childhood relationship you had with your dad.

Most men fear one of four things prior to becoming a father:

(1) They will not be the great father that their dad was.

(2) They will be the bad father that their dad was, and their child will grow up feeling like they do about their dad.

(3) They have never had a father present in their lives, and they are eager to be what they never had. Yet, they haven't seen or even know the first thing about being a father.

(4) And finally, this is a big one: Could they be loved unconditionally despite their weaknesses? This one is the fear that can be present in either of the second or third scenarios that I just mentioned as well.

Circle which scenario or scenarios that best describes you and then tell us why you feel this way.

There are millions of fathers who are dealing with so much hurt from their own childhood that they can't rise up and be fathers for their own children. If you have been knocked down and can't get up, life can be tough. You first have to recognize that there is a difference between getting knocked down and getting knocked out. The difference is one person makes a choice to get up and the other one does not. Have you been knocked down? If your answer is yes then describe the life event that knocked you down.

Often times, many men know when they have been knocked down, but they are not sure if they've gotten up or not. Simply because they are not sure what getting up looks like. Take the time right now to write what getting up looks like to you. How would your life be or look like if you had or were to get up? For example when I saw a picture of what getting up for me would look like. I saw me as a man who had forgiven his own father for his short comings. I saw me calling a man who was a stranger for many years, by a very strange title, Dad. Whether he was deserving or not was another matter. What was important was for me to get up. When I actually had the opportunity to do these things, they were markers or signs that I had gotten up.

Most of us have said it before:

"When I grow up I'm not going to treat my kids like that!"
"When I grow up I'm not going to say hurtful things to my kids like that!"
"I'm not going to ignore my kids like that!"
"I'm not going to let anger destroy my family like that."
"I'm going to love my kids unconditionally!"

Finish the statement the way you did as a child.

"When I grow up I'm not going

To:_____

To:_____

To:_____

To:_____

To:_____

Take note that you have grown up now. By some strange circumstance, have you become the end of your statement? Have you become the father that you said that you would not be?

When you look at yourself in the mirror do you see the man you want your son(s) to be or the man that you want your daughter(s) to marry? If yes why? If no why?

In the book I defined the term The Power of Dad as: The divine influence that God has given to every father to negatively or positively affect their child's life.
It is every man's choice how he uses that God-given influence. He can use it for the good of his children or for the bad. How are you using your power as a dad? Has it been used to impact your child for good or bad? In answering this question it is important that you do not grade yourself by what you intend to do but what you have actually done.

THE POWER OF DAD
NOTES

THE POWER OF DAD
NOTES

CHAPTER TWO

<u>Powerful Roots</u>

My great grandfather's family gave him a nick name "Old Blue." They called him that because he beat his wife until she was black and blue. He will be remembered in infamy by that name even to this day, I don't know his real name. I only know him by the image that he left imprinted on the minds of his children. If your children were to give you a nick name today based on who you are, what you've done, and how you have interacted with them and their mother, what nick name would that be? (Good or Bad)
Why would they call you this?

If it is a negative name what can you do to begin to change your name?

If it is a positive name, what can you do to make sure that you keep that name?

Old Blue was the type of man who could physically protect his family from every and any outside dangers. The only problem was he was the only one causing his family hurt and harm. Blue's dilemma was that he couldn't seem to protect his family from himself. He was the greatest threat to his family both present and future. Let me ask you a question. Have you mastered the art of protecting your child or your family from the hurt and harm of the outside world? Most important, have you learned to protect them from you: your hurtful sarcasm, constant criticism, verbal or physical abuse, lack of attention, mood swings, lack of self control, fears..........etc

It was a reoccurring nightmare! Four generations of intelligent and talented men in my family fail prey to the same flaws of anger and physical abuse. Each one of them suffered unspeakable violence at the hand of their father. And in return grew up and unleashed the same violence upon their families. Have you noticed any common traits in the last two to three generations of men or women in your family? Good or bad. Do you see any of these characteristics in yourself?

The murder of my father's mom was a major event that seemed to shape his life. Can you remember any positive or negative events that seemed to shape your life? Explain what happened and how it shaped your life for the good or bad.

Sometimes the hurt little boy in us never lets us grow up to be the man we want to be. You're a grown man but you still:

Throw fits like a little boy.
Haven't learned to control the anger of the little boy.
Want your father's love.
Wonder why he did what he did.
Wonder where did he go?
Wonder why am I not good enough.
Haven't learned that punching walls only hurts you, the wall doesn't care.
Make decisions with the poor insight of a little boy.
Have not learned to have a deep conversation.
Are still self centered and selfish.
Have not learned to passionately love or to give to others until it hurts.
Wondering why everybody keeps expecting adult things from you when you're just a little boy trapped in an adult's body.

Circle the statements above that most pertains to you.

THE POWER OF DAD
NOTES

THE POWER OF DAD
NOTES

CHAPTER THREE

Powerful Memories, Mirrors & Mentors

Is Father's Day a day of celebration or sadness for you and why?

As a youth:

As an adult (Parent):

Are you a source of joy or sadness for your child (children) on Father's Day and why?

Mirrors are reflective; they show us what we look like and who we are. I've learned that there are situations in life that also act as mirrors which allows us to see ourselves. Through seeing a true reflection of ourselves through these mirrors, we then have the opportunity to make a decision to change what we see in that mirror or to remain the same.

As men we have similar mirrors in our lives. What do the following mirrors tell you about yourself?

1. **Adversity — Your current hardships.**

2. **Success — Your past and/or current achievements.**

3. **Wives/significant others/children— Your family's mental, physical and spiritual well being.**

4. Friends — "Birds of a feather flock together."

5. Finances — Your current financial state.

6. **Purpose — What you have been born to accomplish.**

7. **Privacy — What you do in private.**

8. God's Word — How does God's word reflect who and what you are?

_____
_____
_____
_____
_____
_____
_____
_____
_____
_____
_____

If you're like me, I enjoyed what I saw in some of the mirrors and had some work to do in others. The good news is that these mirrors make us face reality and gives us a chance to choose who we want to be. As stated earlier, the mirror doesn't lie. What you see is what you are. However, what you see does not have to remain the same. When you change, the image in the mirror, will change also.

In my life it was essential for me to remember what happened to me and forget the lessons that were learned lest I followed in my father's footsteps. Each horrific story of my predecessors left me with memories that influenced me. Because I now, too, was a husband and father, this now made me a teacher, and a mentor. In my own personal healing process I found that it was important for me to remember the things that happened to me and then to forget the negative lessons that impacted me. What are some of the things that happened to you that are worth remembering? What lessons are worth forgetting lest you repeat them?

THE POWER OF DAD
NOTES

THE POWER OF DAD
NOTES

CHAPTER FOUR

The Power Of Being Absent

Who's Your Daddy?
In this chapter, we discussed a questionnaire that I would have the youth fill out to determine how well they knew their father's. Let's turn the tables a little bit. How well do you know your child?

Questionnaire
What is your child's or children's favorite color?

What is one of your child's or children's favorite foods?

What do they like to do for fun and relaxation?

What is one of your child's or children's greatest accomplishments or moments?

What is one of your child's or children's greatest disappointments or moments?

What would your child or children say was one of the most memorable moments they had with you? Good and then bad.

What is one of the most hurtful things anyone has ever said or done to your child or children to your knowledge?

What is one of the most encouraging things anyone has ever said or done to your child or children?

What is one of your child's or children's greatest accomplishments?

What would your child or children say was the best and worst thing you ever said to them?

What would your child or children say was one of the best moments they had with you?

What would your child or children say was one of the worst moments they had with you?

What would your child or children say was one of the funniest moments they had with you?

THE POWER OF DAD
NOTES

THE POWER OF DAD
NOTES

CHAPTER FIVE

The Power Of Being There (IDENTITY)

In chapter 5 we discussed identity in detail. The ultimate Father, God, left the rest of us fathers a set of instructions on how to give our children identity.

Acceptance: This is my son.
Affection: Whom I love.
Affirmation: With him I am well pleased.

This is still the blueprint for releasing identity: **A**cceptance, **A**ffection and **A**ffirmation. Keep in mind that identity is always given by one person but always lived out by another. Your child is begging for you to be the one to tell them who they are before someone else does.

Releasing Identity

If you had to tell your kids who they were today, what would you say to release identity over them? Start by using the following statement and structure. To give you a helping hand I started each statement for you.

Statement of Acceptance:

When I look at you I see...

Statement of Affection:

Did I tell you that...?

Statement of Affirmation:

I am proud, excited, honored…..

Remember that this is you leaving your child or children with a, "My daddy said." So this exercise will not be complete until you actually perform it with your children. Go! Follow the steps and the statements that you have written out and begin to change your child's life. I suggest that you begin sharing or speaking these statements today and make it a ritual there after.

We learned that every good mentor mentee relationship has someone who wants to be respected and someone who wants to be accepted. As an adult you probably desire respect from your children and your children desire to be accepted by you. If you can develop these two things in your relationship with your children, then you have an atmosphere to build something wonderful. So what does respect look like to you? In other words what are some ways that your child or children can show respect to you. Further more what are some ways you can show acceptance toward your child or children?

Respecting you looks like:

Respecting you sounds like:

Acceptance looks like to your child or children:
                (You may have to ask them.)

Acceptance sounds like to your child or children:
(You may have to ask them.)

Too often talented, gifted, wise and anointed people take their gifts with them into the next life only to find out that they can't be used there. They're leaving this life with their hands full instead of empty. Name one or two of your talents (abilities) that you're willing to teach someone from the next generation. These are the things that you can leave behind. This will allow you to die empty.

Talent #1:

Talent #2:

THE POWER OF DAD
NOTES

THE POWER OF DAD
NOTES

CHAPTER SIX

The Power Of Communication & Apologies

If you were to write a letter of apology to your child what would it say? Remember that your child's perception is their reality. This means you may be apologizing for something you don't even believe or realize that you've done. But if your child has made it known that you have hurt him or her, then it is their reality and it should be respected. We're not here to win an argument. We are here to win our child's heart. Win the war not the battle. Also keep in mind that the length of time it may take to finish your letter, depends on who you are and the complexities of your relationship. Nevertheless, be committed to follow through with this. It may be the very thing that turns your child's heart towards you. Bottom line, if we're man enough to wound them, let's be man enough to heal them.

The following exercise is designed to help bring healing to your child's heart by simply saying what you are sorry for. It is your chance to write the world's biggest apology to your child for things you have done that may have hurt them. Start with the statement, **"I am sorry for…."** Write things that you want your child to know that you are sorry for. For example: I am sorry for being too busy for you at times. I am sorry for not attending events that were important to you. I am sorry for etc….

The next section of your letter is what **you hope for**. So you will follow the following statement, **"I hope that...."** For example, I hope that you will continue to invite me to your special events. I hope that we can start over etc....

Next your letter will move into one **special moment** that you and your child had together and describe that moment, how you felt, and what you enjoyed about it. For example: I remember teaching you to ride your bike for the first time. I was blessed because you trusted that I would not let you fall. I was so proud when you finally made it down the driveway by yourself. It was one of the joys of my life.

Finally you will end your letter with the section that tells your child **what they mean to you**. For example: I want you to know that you mean the world to me. I want you to know how valuable you are to me.

The next page will give you an opportunity to express your feelings.

The World's Biggest Apology

I'm Sorry For?
_____
_____
_____
_____
_____

You Hope for?
_____
_____
_____
_____
_____

One Special Moment:
_____
_____
_____
_____
_____

What They Mean To You:
_____
_____
_____
_____
_____

Signed _____

Dated _____

THE POWER OF DAD
NOTES

THE POWER OF DAD
NOTES

CHAPTER SEVEN

Kryptonite and Superman

When all the odds were working against him, what did Superman do? He turned the tide. He literally turned back time and faced his greatest fear, the loss of Lois Lane. He was certain that if he did not do anything, he was going to lose the most important relationship in his life. He knew that he would have to fight to restore his relationship. So he faced his fear to gain his prize. What was his fear? Failure. What was the prize? A restored relationship with the love of his life.

Let me make this clear to you. You are Superman. Your child is Lois Lane, the love of your life. Due to circumstances in or out of your control the relationship has died. The walls have caved in on it. An earthquake of disagreements, obstacles, and fears has shaken your relationship to its foundations leaving a chasm too great to cross. The dreams of what you wished you had with your child have crumbled into pieces leaving only ashes. In the aftermath, your child is lost. Your greatest fear has come upon you. You're too late. You've failed. The relationship is dead. You stand there like Superman with tears running from your eyes; you're distraught about what you have lost. At this moment you can throw in the towel and feel sorry for yourself. The other alternative is to dig to the deepest part of you, face your fears, refuse to accept the relationship as it is, and muster up the strength to head towards the stars so that you can turn the tide. What tide will you need to turn or fear will you have to face in order to restore the relationship with your child?

What's your Kryptonite

He was known as the man of steel, and yet his weakness could be found in a pile of green rocks called Kryptonite. Just like him, we all have a form of Kryptonite in our lives. Kryptonite comes in different packages but it always saps your strength and reminds you of your weakness. What is your Kryptonite or weakness? Is it unbridled anger? Maybe it's an insatiable appetite for drugs and alcohol or an overzealous appetite for success. Or maybe it's that horrible thing or those horrible words that you experienced as a child that has never allowed you to fully love others. Maybe it left you so hurt that now your childhood pain is affecting your adulthood destiny. How about your inability to forgive those who have done wrong towards you? Our Kryptonite is the thing that has left us emotionally blind, lame, paralyzed, crippled and disabled. Take the time and contemplate this. It's difficult to change unless you recognize that there is a problem. Start changing the things that you can change. You don't have to pass your Kryptonite down to your children. What is your kryptonite?

Superman's cape represented his strength. With it he was the Man of Steel; without it he was just a man in tights. The cape represents those times that our children look up to us in awe and are proud to say that we are their father. If you are a father who has a poor relationship with your child or children what would you be willing to do to get your cape back? For you dad's who have a great relationship with your children what would you be willing to do to keep your cape?

THE POWER OF DAD
NOTES

THE POWER OF DAD
NOTES

CHAPTER EIGHT

The Power Of The Prodigal

The word prodigal simply means wasteful. So let me ask you a tough question. Have you been a prodigal or wasteful father? To busy with work. Not paying attention. Not taking time. Not being approachable. How are you being a prodigal or wasteful Father?

I can not count how many young people that I have met with prodigal or wasteful fathers. Countless numbers of them are waiting for their dads to come home. Angry? Yes. Hurt? Yes. Yet they were willing to give their father's another chance. In the story of the prodigal father I mentioned some of the emotional obstacles that he had to overcome to restore his relationship with his children, embarrassment, shame and condemnation. The road home is often much longer then the road away from home. What emotional obstacles will you have to overcome on your journey back to your child (ren)? List a few.

THE POWER OF DAD
NOTES

THE POWER OF DAD
NOTES

CHAPTER NINE

The Power Of Love

God commands that we love others as we love ourselves. Sometimes that is the problem. We are loving our children as we love ourselves. The issue is we just don't love ourselves that much. For instance if we have poor self-esteem, we will love our kids through and not around our poor self-esteem.

On a scale of 1-10. One being the lowest and ten being the highest. How would you rate your love for yourself? Then Write why.

      1   2   3   4   5   6   7   8   9   10

If you rated yourself a 7 or less how can you improve?

There are 3 steps we must take in order to learn to love ourselves.

1. **Be Honest With Yourself:** This is a true sign that you are learning to love yourself. You must honestly admit that there are some areas in your life that must change.

2. **Be Patient With Yourself:** Give yourself grace while learning to love yourself. Stop beating yourself up for failing or not measuring up. Soon the patience that you are giving yourself will be the patience that you will freely give to your children.

3. **Be Affirming Towards Yourself:** Maybe you have never had anyone in your life give you affirmation. Your kids may not understand that. All they know is that you are their dad and that they need affirmation from you. Once you are comfortable giving yourself some affirmation it won't be as hard to give it to others.

Which of these steps can you begin to work on today that will help you learn to love yourself?

What is love? We all have different thoughts and opinions to this question. Ask your child or children to give you their personal definition of the word love. Better yet, ask them what are two things that make them feel loved. Now write down your own personal definition of the word love and two things that make you feel loved. Then compare your list with your child's or children's list.

Write down some ways that you can show your child or children love the way he/she has defined it.

Derrick Redmond was a sprinter in the 1992 Barcelona Olympics. During the biggest race of his life he collapsed as he headed towards the finish line. Just when it seemed that he would not even finish the race, something amazing happened. His father made his way through the crowd and past security to help his son finish the race. Derrick's father was determined to help him reach his goal of crossing the finish line. This was the defining moment of the 1992 Olympics. Name two people, like Derrick Redmond's father, who have helped you reach your dreams and goals. How did they help you reach those goals?

What are some of your children's goals? How can you help them accomplish their goals?

THE POWER OF DAD
NOTES

THE POWER OF DAD
NOTES

CHAPTER TEN

The Fight Of Your Life

The average daily amount of one-to-one father/child contact reported in this country is less than 30 minutes a day. What activities or hobbies are your children involved in that would allow you to spend more time with them? Remember you are in the fight of your life. So find a way to win.

**THE POWER OF DAD
NOTES**

THE POWER OF DAD
NOTES

CHAPTER ELEVEN

Following & Fighting

Your child will likely walk in your foot steps morally, ethically, spiritually and maybe even occupationally. Are you proud of the trail that you have blazed or does this thought strike fear in your heart?

What does the youth of this nation want? They want to hear us say, "Your father is paying attention and desires to bless you. You are enough; you don't have to keep trying to be someone else. You are no longer next in line, but you are now at the front of the line." Is there is something or someone in your life that makes your child(ren) feel like a low priority? What or who do you think these things or people are?

I believe that I am passing down morals, work ethics, and a belief system that will possibly effect the next 500 years of my family. I constantly ask myself, "What is my 500 year plan?" The life that I am living and the decisions that I am making could determine the well being and the character of my family for generations. Since my life has this type of an impact, I better be very intentional about the impact that I leave. Let me ask you, what is your 500 year plan? In other words, what are the core values habits, morals, ethics and/or spiritual truths that you want to impact your generations?

How will you implement your 500 year plan and make an impact?

THE POWER OF DAD
NOTES

THE POWER OF DAD
NOTES

About The Author

Brian Pruitt is the Founder and CEO of Brian Pruitt Motivational.

Brian is an international Motivational Speaker who inspires youth and adults to overcome obstacles and accomplish their dreams.

Brian Graduated from Central Michigan University in 1995 with a Bachelor's Degree in Communications. A gifted athlete, Brian Played football for CMU and in 1994 was named AP First Team All American. He has subsequently been inducted into the CMU Sports Hall of Fame. He has also been inducted into the Saginaw County Hall of Fame in Saginaw, Michigan.

Mr. Pruitt has traveled across this country and others challenging and teaching listeners to overcome obstacles and accomplish their dreams. In addition, he has been a regional presenter for Youth Alive-7 Project, and has been featured guest on several television programs. Brian has been honored as a key note speaker for well known ministries such as Teen Mania. He has served as a Motivational Speaker and Life Coach for youth, adults, church's, sports teams, and businesses throughout the U.S, Canada, Mexico, and Sweden.

As an Author, Successful Entrepreneur, and Television Personality Brian's message is reaching the world and igniting passion. Brian and his wife, Delicia have been married for over twelve years and have two daughters, Brianna Joy & Destiny Danae. They reside in Saginaw, Michigan.

For More Information, Books, Clothing, CD's and DVD's From Brian Pruitt Motivational (BPM)

Please check out our web site located at:

www.brianpruittmotivational.com
OR
www.haccman.com

Contact Brian Pruitt to speak at your next event.

If you would like Brian Pruitt to come and speak at your next event here are a few ways to contact us. Brian is great for:

Corporate Meetings
Church's
Colleges
School Assemblies
Sports Teams
Men's Conferences
Youth Conferences
You name it! Brian Pruitt Motivational is your fit.

Address:
Brian Pruitt Motivational
P.O. Box 294
Saginaw, MI 48606

Phone: (989) 249-0951

E-Mail: brianpruitt41@hotmail.com
Or contact@haccman.com

To find out more about Brian Pruitt Motivational please go to our web site.

www.haccman.com
OR
www.brianpruittmotivational.com

www.ingramcontent.com/pod-product-compliance
Ingram Content Group UK Ltd.
Pitfield, Milton Keynes, MK11 3LW, UK
UKHW041956230426
12048UKWH00008B/372